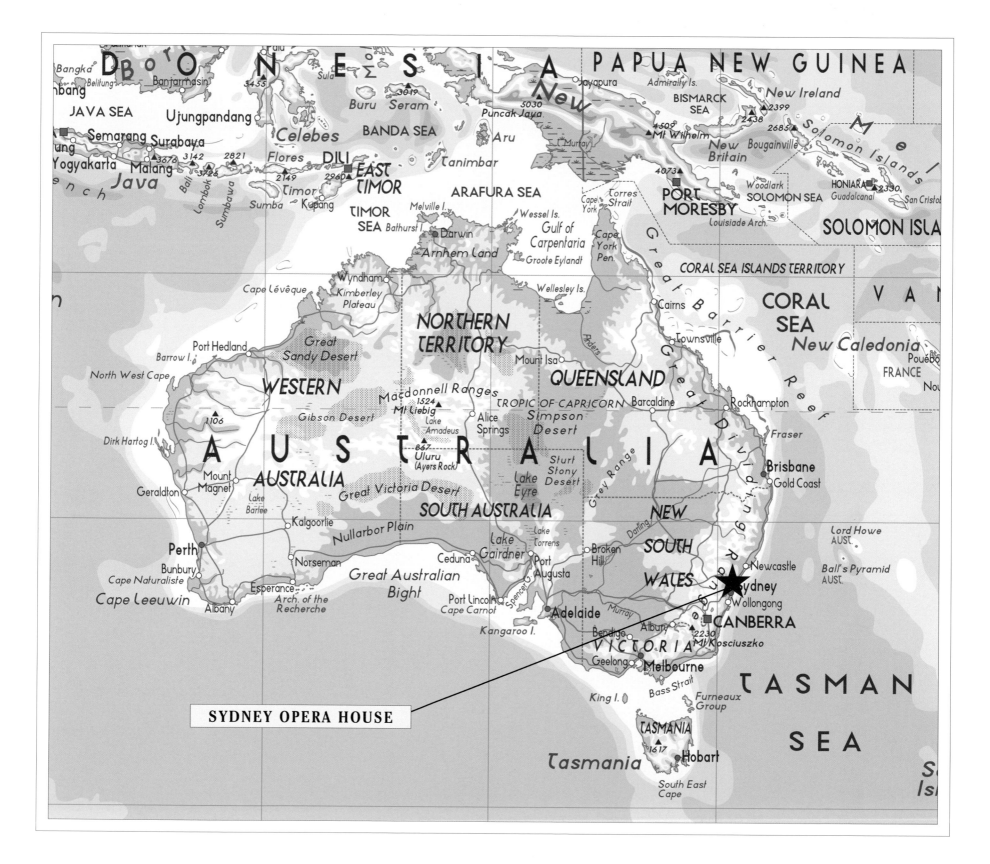

SYDNEY OPERA HOUSE

Published by Creative Education
123 South Broad Street
Mankato, Minnesota 56001

Creative Education is an imprint of The Creative Company.

Designed by Stephanie Blumenthal
Production design by Melinda Belter
Art direction by Rita Marshall

Photographs by Alamy (Bill Bachmann, David Ball, Cephas Picture Library, Christine Osborne Pictures, Darroch Donald, david sanger photography, Steven Dusk, Chad Ehlers, eye35.com, Peter Fakler, Food Features, geogphotos, Simon Grosset, david hancock, James Davis Photography, Andre Jenny, Sean O'Neill, POPPERFOTO, Rolf Richardson, DY Riess MD, doug steley, Stock Connection, Jack Sullivan, Greg Vaughn, Mireille Vautier, WorldFoto, S.T. Yiap), Design Maps, Inc., Getty Images (altrendo travel, Keystone, Harvey Lloyd, Dominic Harcourt Webster, Simon Wilkinson)

Printed in the United States of America

Library of Congress Cataloging-in-Publication Data
Shofner, Shawndra.
Sydney Opera House / by Shawndra Shofner.
p. cm. — (Modern wonders of the world)
Includes index.
ISBN-13: 978-1-58341-442-2
1. Sydney Opera House—Juvenile literature. 2. Utzon, Jorn, 1918—Juvenile literature. 3. Sydney (N.S.W.)—Buildings, structures, etc.—Juvenile literature. I. Title. II. Series.

NA6840.A79S972 2006   725'.822'09441—dc22   2005050665

First edition

2 4 6 8 9 7 5 3 1

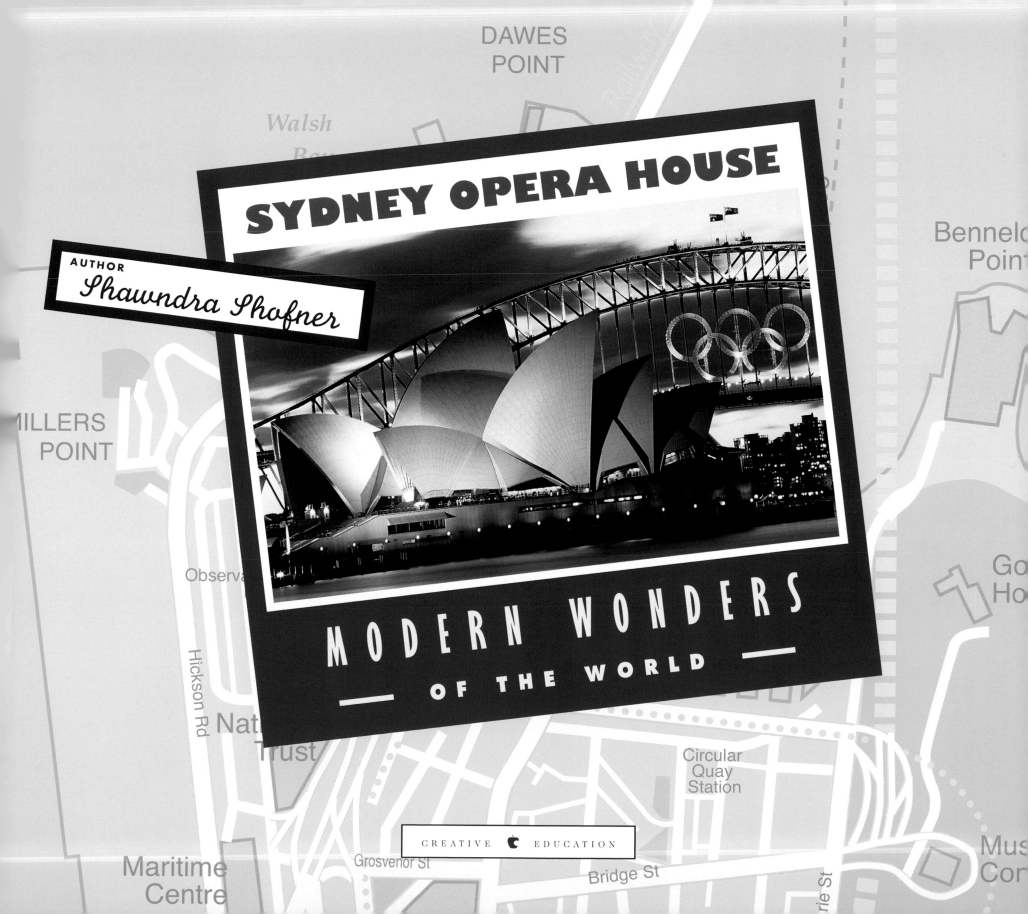

SYDNEY OPERA HOUSE

AUTHOR
Shawndra Shofner

MODERN WONDERS
OF THE WORLD

CREATIVE ☕ EDUCATION

Although not the tallest structure in the city, the Sydney Opera House is certainly the most distinctive, its unique, sail-shaped roofs harmonizing perfectly with the surrounding harbor.

Waves from the Pacific Ocean splash on rocks near what at first glance appears to be an enormous ship. The steel arches of the nearby Sydney Harbor Bridge point the way out to sea, but this ship will never set sail. This magnificent structure, recognizable by roofs that look like huge sails cupping the breeze, is the Sydney Opera House, an Australian performing arts complex so masterfully designed that its concrete, granite, wood, and glass form appears to rock gently on the harbor waters alongside ferries, boats, and yachts. Even though it was born less than 50 years ago, the Sydney Opera House has become as much a symbol of Australia as the kangaroo and koala.

A DREAM REALIZED

Most Australian cities are located along the continent's shore. The desert-like inland area of Australia is called the "Outback." Kangaroos, emus, wedgetail eagles, geckos, and king brown snakes make this wild country their home, as do white daisies, scarlet desert peas, and yellow cassia flowers.

Britain founded the coastal city of Sydney, in the eastern Australian state of New South Wales, as a **penal colony** in 1788. To ease crowded conditions in their jails, the British transported criminals convicted of minor crimes such as petty theft, street fighting, or overdue debt to Sydney until 1840. When gold was discovered in nearby Wellington County in 1851, dreams of striking it rich attracted thousands of immigrants to the continent, just as the gold rush of 1849 brought people to California. By the early 20th century, Sydney had shed its image as a convict community and become a bustling modern city populated by almost 500,000 people from more than 180 nations.

After World War II ended in 1945, many Europeans left their war-ravaged homelands and moved to Australia, swelling Sydney's population to more than one million. The construction of new homes, businesses, schools, churches, and stores boomed. Citizens soon hungered for entertainment such as orchestra concerts, live **opera**, and dramatic theater, but Sydney lacked suitable performance spaces.

In 1954, Eugene Goosens, chief conductor of the Sydney Symphony Orchestra, met with Joseph Cahill, **premier** of New South Wales, to discuss the creation of a modern, multipurpose concert hall in

6

Music has been popular since ancient times, when instruments such as didgeradoos (opposite center) and Australian hardwood music sticks (opposite right) were played. When English-born conductor Eugene Goosens (left) took over the Sydney Symphony Orchestra, he longed for a grand performance hall for his musicians.

At the time 38-year-old Jorn Utzon—who had studied architecture at the Academy of Arts in Copenhagen, Denmark— learned about the Sydney Opera House Design contest, he was running his own architectural firm and designing mainly private residences.

Sydney. Soon afterward, Cahill created a government advisory board called the Opera House Committee and charged it with getting such a building project underway.

For the building's site, the committee selected a section of the city's waterfront along Bennelong Point, a **peninsula** that jutted into the Sydney Harbor and housed a rundown garage filled with idle trolleys, or electric rail cars. The committee then discussed ideas for a building that could accommodate a variety of events. It decided on a building that would include one large hall big enough to host **symphony**, opera, ballet, dance, and choir performances, as well as pageants and conferences, and one small hall for theater, intimate opera, **chamber music**, concerts, recitals, and lectures. The committee decided to try to attract designs by talented architects from around the world. On February 15, 1956, it announced an international competition, with a cash award of $5,000 for the winning design.

Halfway across the world, in his studio in Hellebaek, Denmark, a 38-year-old amateur architect named Jorn Utzon read about the competition in a Swedish architecture journal. Intrigued, he studied photographs, postcards, and naval charts of Bennelong Point. The rolling waters, gliding sailboats, and stunning metropolitan skyline he saw piqued his interest, and he sent for the guidelines.

Sydney Harbor, widely regarded as one of the most beautiful natural harbors in the world, runs between the northern and southern halves of Sydney. The harbor has long been a center of both recreation and commerce.

Architect Eero Saarinen, who was instrumental in the choice of Jorn Utzon's design for the Sydney Opera House, was known for creating unusual buildings, including the Gateway Arch (below) in St. Louis, Missouri. Utzon's winning design included steep stairs (right) leading up the building.

In a stroke of luck, Utzon met some women from Sydney while at the 1956 Olympics in Stockholm, Sweden. Their enthusiastic description of their native city and its harbor inspired the architect. He created and submitted for consideration billowing sketches that were influenced by many things, including his own sailing experience, the Mayan pyramids at Chichen Itza in Mexico, and Kronborg Castle on the Atlantic coast at Helsingør, Denmark.

Utzon's design proposal was one of 233 from 27 different countries. The panel of judges assembled to select the winning design included two Australians: New South Wales government architect

Cobden Parkes, and Henry Ingham Ashworth, a professor of architecture at the University of Sydney. It also included two international judges: Leslie Martin, chief architect of the London Country Council, and Eero Saarinen, an acclaimed Finnish-American architect from Michigan.

Saarinen arrived in Sydney three days after the other judges convened. While thumbing through the pile of entries his fellow judges had rejected, one unusual design caught his attention. He urged the other judges to reconsider it, pointing out how its sail-like roofs complemented the harbor site. On January 29, 1957, Premier Cahill announced the winning entry. It came from Denmark and belonged to Jorn Utzon.

10

Like the Sydney Opera House, Kronborg Castle (top), in Jorn Utzon's homeland of Denmark, was built on the water. The immense structure, constructed in the mid-1570s, inspired Utzon's design for the opera house, as did the stepped pyramid (bottom) at Chichen Itza, Mexico, built by the Maya around 800 A.D.

CONSTRUCTION AND CONTROVERSY

The Sydney Opera House is built on land that once belonged to Australia's native people, the Aborigines. Captain Arthur Phillip, who landed with Britain's first shipload of convict settlers in Sydney Cove in 1788, befriended an Aborigine named Bennelong, whose name was given to Bennelong Point.

The New South Wales government projected that the Sydney Opera House would take four years to build and cost $7 million in Australian currency (about $4.7 million in United States currency). When an **appeal fund** brought in less than $1 million, Premier Joseph Cahill arranged to raise the money through a **lottery**.

In 1959, workers tore down the trolley garage on Bennelong Point and began building the podium, a cement platform 607 feet (185 m) long and 388 feet (120 m) wide on which the opera house would stand. After the work had begun, the government ordered that the number of performance halls be increased from two to four—a demand that required Jorn Utzon to draw up new designs matching the government's latest specifications. Further complicating matters was the fact that no one yet knew if the design's most dramatic feature—its massive, sail-like roofs—could even be built.

Utzon spent four years researching means of constructing the roofs. One day, after gazing at an orange and its segments, Utzon had a breakthrough. He assigned each roof shell the same geometric curve, as if they were each cut out of a sphere. His calculations showed that construction workers could create the roof vaults, or arches, by making cement ribs in molds onsite, lifting

As Jorn Utzon saw the roof sails on the Sydney Opera House take shape, he declared, "I have made a sculpture." From the time he had submitted his original design for the building, Utzon realized that a structure on a site as exposed as Bennelong Point would require a spectacular roof.

On March 18, 2003, two men climbed to the top of the Sydney Opera House's highest roof sail and painted "No War" in red paint to protest against the invasion of Iraq by the militaries of America, Britain, and other nations. The vandalism was quickly cleaned off at an expense of $151,000, and security around the building was increased.

them into place by crane, and then gluing them together. The only drawback to this method was that the new curves changed the building's appearance. The *Sydney Morning Herald* soon published an illustration that showed the roofs at a more upright angle than that in the award-winning design. The picture shocked and worried a public that was already skeptical of the project due to its delays and rising costs.

To top it all off, the construction crew had to abruptly stop work on the roof vaults in 1962 when engineers realized that the podium would not be able to support the 26,800-ton (24,360 t), re-designed roof shells. The roof support columns, which passed through the podium deep into the lower foundation, had to be demolished and replaced with stronger ones that were eight feet square (2.4 sq m) in size.

In a ploy to avoid more bad press, workers tried to complete the new work in secret, blasting only during Sydney's afternoon rush hour so that traffic noise would mask the blasts. When an explosion threw a chunk of concrete into the air and onto a passing ferry, however, headlines quickly tattled.

Before long, Robert Askin campaigned for the position of premier of New South Wales by promising to control the opera house's spiraling costs and construction

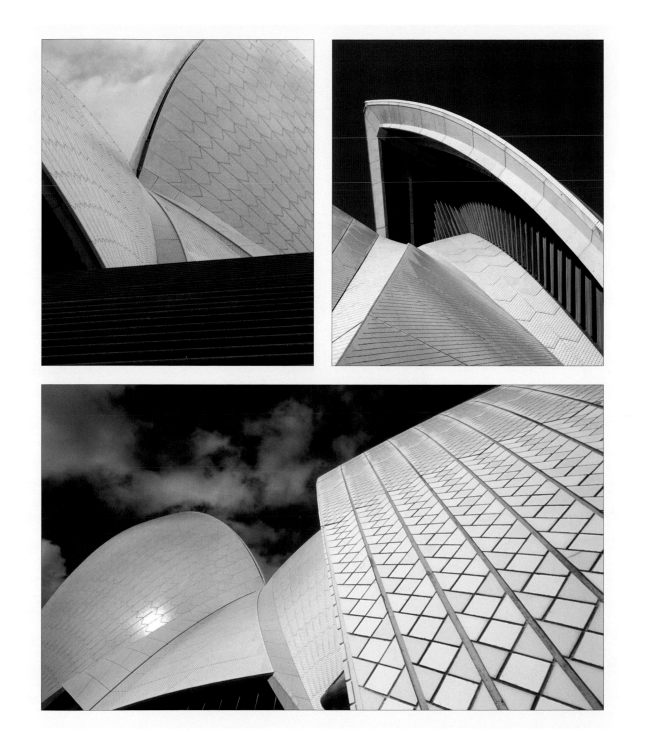

The roof sails of the Sydney Opera House glisten with 1,056,000 white and cream tiles imported from Sweden. Inspectors periodically examine and replace the roof tiles, then enjoy the exhilaration of rappelling down from the roofs' heights (opposite).

Australia's natural timber and granite (right) enhance the Sydney Opera House's interior, while the setting sun beautifies its exterior.

delays. He was elected premier in 1965 and soon restricted Utzon's freedom to choose **subcontractors**, withheld payments, and required government authorization of all designs and construction methods. Frustrated by the interference, Utzon resigned from the project—which to that point had cost $18 million—in February 1966 and left Australia forever.

Askin and the New South Wales government hired Australian architects Peter Hall, Lionel Todd, and David Littlemore to take over where Utzon had left off. Over the next seven years, the architects managed crews that completed the roofs and finished off more than 1,000 interior rooms with a combination of natural materials from New South Wales. Stairs and walkways displayed **granite** from a mine in nearby Tarama, flooring and walls featured warm, rich brush box wood, and ceiling beams cascaded down in white birch.

At a cost of seven years and more than $80 million, this final phase of construction broke Premier Askin's campaign promises to limit the project's time and cost. Nevertheless, by October 1973, the great Sydney Opera House, a most unique structure designed to complement the harbor on the outside and offer world-class performance spaces on the inside, was finally finished.

AUSTRALIA'S MODERN ICON

Although the Sydney Opera House is usually bustling with activity, an early morning stroll reveals the venue's more tranquil side.

The Sydney Opera House officially opened on October 20, 1973. England's Queen Elizabeth II was present for the opening, and thousands of people celebrated by taking in free music, dance performances, and an evening fireworks display. For the next two years, enthusiastic Australians purchased enough lottery tickets for the government to pay off the building's price tag of $102 million by July 1975.

Expensive as it was, just 14 years after the opera house opened, it needed an additional $86 million worth of repairs to fix fallen roof tiles and leaks in the roof, windows, and walls. Today, the New South Wales government pays for approximately 30 percent of the building's maintenance, remodeling, and operating costs. Business partnerships, corporate sponsors, and sales of officially licensed Sydney Opera House merchandise fund the rest.

In the late 1980s, the Sydney Opera House received two additions: a two-level walkway along the building's west side, and a fifth theater, called the Playhouse. In response to increasingly crowded parking conditions on streets adjacent to the opera house, a 1,100-car parking garage was also constructed in 1993 underneath the nearby Royal Botanic Gardens.

In 1999, the Opera House Trust, a government agency that has operated and maintained the Sydney Opera House since

Between 1969 and 1979, Australian Ronald Sharp designed and built the Grand Organ for the Sydney Opera House's Concert Hall. Containing 10,500 pipes, it is the largest mechanical pipe organ in the world. Recordings are sold of classical music played on the Grand Organ by Australian organist Michael Dudman.

The Sydney Opera House offers performances of all kinds, including operas and recitals on the Grand Organ (opposite).

1961, made the decision that ongoing and future renovations should be made under the direction of the building's original architect. The agency invited Jorn Utzon, then 78 years old, to be involved with the project once again. He accepted. From his cliff-top home on the Spanish island of Majorca, Utzon immediately went to work. Since he no longer traveled, his son, Jan, and Australian architect Richard Johnson were placed in charge of all onsite work.

Utzon soon developed a plan that outlined more than $69 million worth of immediate improvements and updates to the opera house. These changes included making the complex accessible to the handicapped, extending the Opera Theater orchestra pit, modernizing the Opera Theater auditorium and the Concert Hall, and constructing a glass **colonnade** to connect the harbor-facing western lobbies. Utzon also detailed his architectural vision for the future of the Sydney Opera House, putting in place long-term guidelines to ensure that any renovations yet to come will complement his masterful design even after his death.

The opera house's Reception Hall was the first part of the building to be remodeled under Utzon's direction. The green carpet and dance floor were recovered in Tasmanian

The interior halls are not the only usable performance space offered by the Sydney Opera House. On New Year's Eve in 1999, the roof sails provided dance space for six members of the Australian Dance Theater, athletic performing space for Circus Oz acrobats, and seating space for musicians accompanying a choir.

blue gum timber, and discolored wooden fixtures and tarnished fittings were replaced with white birch and bronze. One of Utzon's personal additions to the hall was a multicolored wool wall hanging that he designed himself. The room was renamed the Utzon Room in honor of the distinguished architect.

In April 2003, Jorn Utzon received the Pritzker Prize, the most prestigious architectural award in the world. The annual Pritzker, established in 1979 by the developers of the Hyatt hotel chain, honors an architect whose vision and work continues to affect humanity and its environment. The Sydney Opera House itself was similar-

ly honored in 2005. As a reflection of its architectural, historical, and cultural importance, the Sydney Opera House was added to Australia's National Heritage List, giving the building protected status as a national landmark.

The people of Sydney, Australia, and the world are treated to more than 3,000 different performances a year at the Sydney Opera House. Fulfilling the dreams of founders Eugene Goosens and Joseph Cahill, the opera house has become one of the most revered, photographed, and celebrated performing arts centers in the world. And despite its turbulent beginnings, this sculpture-like building, appearing at all times about to set sail, has become a modern icon of Australia.

Because it is situated just west of the **international date line**, Australia was one of the first countries to welcome the millennium in 2000. More than 16,000 people attended a free party in front of the Sydney Opera House and watched a fireworks display launched from the house's shells at midnight.

From its lobbies (opposite) bathed in natural light to its roof shells illuminated by the glow of fireworks, the Sydney Opera House is a feast for the eyes.

SEEING THE WONDER

The Sydney Opera House attracts more than 4.5 million visitors from around the world every year. After arriving in Sydney, Australia's largest city, visitors may reach the Sydney Opera House by train, bus, ferry, or taxi. Many tourists buy the SydneyPass sightseeing package, which varies in cost and allows unlimited travel on all modes of public transportation.

The Sydney Opera House is open 363 days a year (closed only on Christmas Day and Good Friday). Visitors can take guided one-hour tours, which begin every half hour between 9:00 A.M. and 5:00 P.M. As of 2006, ticket prices ranged from $23 for one adult to $64 for a family of four. For a more thorough experience, visitors can pay about $140 for a backstage tour that allows them to stand on stages, go down into the orchestra pit, and visit a dressing room for performers. Reservations are required for this once-daily tour, which begins at 7:00 A.M.

For visitors interested in experiencing not only the building but its arts and music, the Sydney Opera House offers performance packages. Visitors may attend any performance, such as a concert or ballet, and select a dinner, souvenir gift, or cruise. Prices vary, and reservations are required. The Sydney Opera House's official Web site

The Metro Monorail (opposite) is one of the most popular ways to get around Sydney. Tourists lucky enough to visit at the right time can watch as stunning ships cruise through Sydney Harbor (top). For those who want to get closer to the water, several companies offer harbor cruises.

Among Australia's most popular foods are Sydney rock oysters, fried kangaroo fillets, flake (shark meat), chips (French fries), cuppa (cup of tea), and for dessert, either a coconut jam tart or Pavlova, a meringue- and cream-filled dessert of passion fruit and banana.

Like the white ibis (right) and Pavlova (far right), the Sydney Opera House is uniquely Australian.

(www.sydneyoperahouse.com) posts dates, times, and reservation information for all performances and programs.

Sydney has a mild climate and is located in the southern hemisphere at a latitude similar to that of Los Angeles, California, in the northern hemisphere. Summer in Australia occurs from December through February and features average temperatures of 77 °F (22 °C). The winter months of June, July, and August are mild, averaging 55 °F (13 °C). The ocean breeze can make the air feel cooler,

however, and visitors are encouraged to bring a jacket regardless of the season.

Many tourists who visit the Sydney Opera House also check out the Royal Botanic Gardens, which are only a short walk away and offer a wide sampling of Australia's native plant and animal life. Above waratah flowers and paper daisies, white ibis birds and flying foxes flit among the foliage of Australian gum trees, while brush-tailed possums scurry about making nests. More Australian animals, including the platypus and little penguin, can be seen at the nearby Taronga Park Zoo.

QUICK FACTS

Location: Sydney, Australia, on Bennelong Point

Time of construction: March 1959 to October 1973

Opening date: October 20, 1973; the opening celebration was attended by Queen Elizabeth II and featured fireworks and a performance of Ludwig van Beethoven's Ninth Sympony

Composition: Concrete, granite, and glass

Architects: Jorn Utzon (principal designer), Peter Hall, Lionel Todd, and David Littlemore

Work force involved: ~ 1,350

Height (at highest roof vault): 230 feet (70 m)

Width: 388 feet (118 m)

Length: 605 feet (185 m)

Capacity: ~ 5,000 people

Cost to build: $66 million ($102 million in Australian currency) at time of completion

Funded by: The Australian public using profits from a government-run lottery

Nicknames: The Concrete Camel, Hunchback of Bennelong Point

Annual visitors: ~ 4.5 million

GLOSSARY

appeal fund — a fund-raising campaign designed to attract money from a variety of sources, including businesses and individual citizens, to pay for a specific project

chamber music — music performed by small groups in a small room or hall

colonnade — a series of columns that support a roof structure and may form a walkway

granite — a very hard kind of rock produced by intense heat underground; it is usually grayish pink in color

international date line — the imaginary north-south line on Earth that separates two consecutive days

lottery — a fund-raising game in which tickets are sold and the profits are split between the sponsor and a person whose ticket numbers match numbers drawn

opera — a theatrical play in which all lines are sung to the accompaniment of music; "intimate opera" is such a play performed before a small audience

penal colony — a city or area in which convicted criminals are sent to live

peninsula — a piece of land surrounded by water on three sides

premier — the top state government official, similar to a prime minister; in Australia, the position is similar to state governors in the United States

subcontractors — companies or people hired by a project supervisor to construct specific parts of a building, such as the foundation or roof

symphony — a classical, instrumental form of music usually performed by an orchestra, or large collection of musicians

INDEX